Street Art & Painted Moments

ADULT COLORING BOOK WITH POETRY AND SELF-DISCOVERY

Aventuras De Viaje

Copyright SF Nonfiction Books © 2024

All Rights Reserved

No part of this document may be reproduced without written consent from the author.

www.SFNonfictionBooks.com

INTRODUCTION

Welcome to the vivid streets where art bursts in color and life, where the pulse of creativity flows through every painted wall and whispered verse. This isn't just a coloring book—it's an exploration, a retreat, and a tribute to the boundless spirit of street art and poetic discovery.

Each page invites you deeper into the urban landscape, where intricate murals, sprawling graffiti, and poetic inscriptions transform ordinary spaces into canvases of personal expression. These creations, symbols of resilience, innovation, and the vibrant pulse of city life, wait for your palette to bring them into full bloom. Coloring these scenes offers not only a visual journey but also an intimate engagement with the soul of the streets.

In our daily rush, finding a moment to simply be present is priceless. This book offers you a chance to slow down, to dive into a world of color and contemplation, and to reconnect with the communal heartbeat of urban artistry. It's a call to revive your inner child's wonder and paint it with a spectrum of emotions.

Dive into this artistic adventure, immersing yourself in the layers of street art and the meditative act of coloring. Here, you're not just passing through a scenery; you're engaging with a culture, awakening your creativity, and embracing the tranquility of artistic mindfulness.

Discovering the Mosaic of Imagination

Dive deeper, and you'll find that this book has been meticulously crafted to enhance your personal journey:

- **Simple Activities:** Beyond just coloring, engage with activities designed to spark reflection and creativity. These gentle prompts will lead you to moments of introspection, serving as kindling for your inner fire.

- **Quotes:** Let the wisdom of personal development accompany you, illuminating your path as you add your own burst of color to the pages.

- **Positive Affirmations:** As you color, let these words of positivity uplift your spirit, molding your thoughts and inspiring a brighter perspective.

- **Poems and Haikus**: Delight in the poetic tales that complement the theme of this book, capturing life's varied rhythms and experiences. Each verse and every line serve as a muse for your artistic endeavors, enhancing your coloring journey with lyrical inspiration.

Embark on this coloring odyssey, immersing yourself in a world of diverse themes and the therapeutic embrace of art. Each page invites you on a unique journey, blending your creativity with the tranquility of coloring.

THANKS FOR YOUR PURCHASE

Get Your Next SF Nonfiction Book FREE!

Claim the book of your choice at:

www.SFNonfictionBooks.com/Free-Book

You will also be among the first to know of all the latest releases, discount offers, bonus content, and more.

Go to:

www.SFNonfictionBooks.com/Free-Book

Thanks again for your support.

Daily Blessing:
What made you smile today?

_____

_____

"Art enables us to find ourselves and lose ourselves at the same time."
— Thomas Merton

I create beauty through my challenges.

In city's heart where colors play,
Dreams sketch the lines of a brighter day.

Personal Masterpiece:
Which color represents your current mood and why?

_____

_____

"Creativity takes courage."
— Henri Matisse

I see the world as a canvas of opportunities.

Spray cans hiss,
Walls bloom—city's canvas
Unfurls in color.

Street Art Surprise:
Describe a piece of street art that has impacted you recently.

_____

_____

"Every artist was first an amateur."
— Ralph Waldo Emerson

I embrace my unique perspective.

Along these urban trails we find,
Our own selves in the paints entwined.

Creative Moments:
What creativity did you bring into your day?

_____

_____

"In the world of art, all things are possible."

— *Unknown*

I am inspired by the vibrancy around me.

Bold mural strokes,
Whisper tales of concrete
—Voices painted.

Colors of Life:
Which colors do you feel most grateful for today?

_____

_____

"Art is not what you see, but what you make others see."

— *Edgar Degas*

I am a masterpiece in progress.

Each stroke a word, each color a song,
Art's dialogue, where we all belong.

Words on Walls:
If you could write a message on a wall, what would it be?

_____

_____

"The urge to destroy is also a creative urge."
— Pablo Picasso

I am connected to the endless creativity of the universe.

Street corner muse,
Art speaks in silent hues—
Listen deeply.

Poetry in Motion:
Write a short poem about the pace of your life.

_____

_____

"I dream my painting and I paint my dream."
— *Vincent van Gogh*

I color my life with joy and gratitude.

Art's fleeting stroke on brick-stained wall,
Captures the spirit of fall and sprawl.

Reflections of the City:
What part of your city inspires you the most?

_____

_____

"An artist cannot fail; it is a success to be one."
— *Charles Cooley*

I trust in my ability to create wonder.

Shadows dance,
On walls, lives narrate—
Night's art whispers.

Urban Harmony:
How does your environment
influence your mood?

_____

_____

"Creativity is allowing yourself to make mistakes. Art is knowing which ones to keep."
— *Scott Adams*

I embrace change as a pathway to growth.

Where ink meets wall, the world takes note,
Our stories stay, in paint they float.

A World of Textures:
Describe a texture you felt today
and your thoughts about it.

_____

_____

"Creativity is intelligence having fun."

— *Albert Einstein*

I am the curator of my own gallery.

Urban canvas,
Life in vibrant swatches—
Palette of dreams.

Emotions Palette:
Which emotions did you paint your day with?

_____

_____

"A true artist is not one who is inspired, but one who inspires others."

— *Salvador Dalí*

I am unstoppable in my artistic journey.

On streets we roam,
In art we trust,
Finding ourselves in layers of dust.

Patterns of Thought:
Identify a recurring thought and explore its texture.

_____

_____

"To create one's own world takes courage."
— Georgia O'Keeffe

I transform the ordinary into extraordinary.

Graffiti soul,
Sprawled stories in color—
City breathes art.

The Art of Listening:
Whom did you really listen to today?

_____

_____

"Creativity is breaking out of established patterns to look at things in a different way."
— Edward de Bono

BEYOND THESE PAGES

A Deeper Dive into Art and Soul Awaits!

This book is but a chapter in a voyage where creativity meets depth.

Craving more? Explore the link below and weave deeper into the tapestry of art and emotion.

www.SFNonfictionBooks.com/Adult-Coloring-Books

A HEARTFELT THANK YOU

As the colors on these pages have come to life, so has our shared journey in this artistic realm. I am deeply grateful for your trust in choosing this book, and more so for allowing it to be a part of your self-care and personal journey.

Taking time for oneself is a gift—a silent promise of growth, introspection, and rejuvenation. By picking up the colors and filling these pages, you've not just created art but have also woven moments of peace, reflection, and creativity into your life.

Thank you for making space for yourself, for embracing the wonders within these pages, and for dancing to the rhythm of the lines and hues within this book. Your journey here is a testament to the beauty of dedicating time to one's soul and spirit.

If you enjoyed this journey and wish to explore more, know that there are other themes awaiting your artistic touch. Dive into new worlds and let your imagination flow.

From the deepest corner of my heart, thank you for bringing this book to life. Until our next artistic adventure together, cherish the colors of your journey and continue to shine.

Warmly,

Aventuras De Viaje

ABOUT THE AUTHOR

Aventuras has three passions: travel, writing, and learning new skills.

Combining these three things, Miss Viaje spends her time exploring the world and learning about anything and everything that interests her, from yoga, to music, to science, and more.

Aventuras takes what she discovers and shares it through her books.

www.SFNonfictionBooks.com

www.ingramcontent.com/pod-product-compliance
Lightning Source LLC
Chambersburg PA
CBHW081621100526
44590CB00021B/3544